LOVE MIXED WITH LOVE!

Mommy & Me in the Kitchen.

Mixes, Recipes, Gifts & Ideas for each month of the year!

© Copyright 2000, Sheryl Lynn's
ISBN 0-615-113302-3

Written and illustrated by
Patricia Buck & Sheryl Lynn Johnson

Printed in the USA. on recycled paper...

January

Make copies of these labels for your gift tags!

Idea!

HAPPY NEW YEAR!

Let the kids collect tin cans. Wash and remove labels. Spray paint in bright colors. Punch 2 holes in top and thread wire for handles. Paint "HAPPY NEW YEAR". You can also paint on old pans & lids you've collected at garage sales. Use old spoons to bang with... CELEBRATE!

2   MIXED WITH LOVE!

HOT CHOCOLATE MIX

1½ c. powdered milk
⅓ c. sugar
¼ c. cocoa
Mix together and place in an air-tight container.

to:

from:

let it snow!

HOT CHOCOLATE

Fill mug with 4 T. hot chocolate mix. Pour boiling water in mug and stir. Top with marshmallows or whipped cream. Enjoy!

let it snow!

Packaging IDEAS:

* Place mix in a sealed bag and put inside a pretty mug. Tie on label, candy cane dipped in chocolate, or cinnamon stick stirrer!

··· OR ···

* Fill a pair of mittens with bags of mix, tie with ribbon and label!

MIXED WITH LOVE! 3

Chili Mix

2 t. cumin
2 t. oregano
½ t. salt
½ t. cayenne pepper

2 t. onion powder
½ t. garlic powder
⅓ c. masa harina
1 T. chili powder

Mix together ingredients and place in an air-tight container. Old spice jars are great containers. Just spray paint lids. Tie up Chili Mix with a red bandana and attach label.

Chili

2 T. oil
2 pounds ground beef
1 package chili mix
1 16 oz. can chopped tomatoes
2 cups water

In a Dutch oven brown beef in oil until it's not pink. Add the next 3 ingredients and simmer for 30 minutes. Serve with chopped onions, grated cheese and a dollup of sour cream.

THE BEST Cornbread Mix

2 c. Bisquick™
½ c. cornmeal
½ c. sugar
1 T. baking powder

Mix with love and place in an air-tight container. Attach label →

BEAN SOUP MIX

1 lb. navy beans	1 lb. pinto beans
1 lb. great Northern beans	1 lb. red beans
1 lb. black beans	1 lb. lima beans
1 lb. black-eyed peas	1 lb. yellow split peas
1 lb. dried lentils	1 lb. green split peas
1 lb. barley pearls	

• Combine all beans in large bowl and mix with love! Measure out 2 cup gift packages into cellophane bags or glass jars. Makes approx. 20 packages

---

BEAN SOUP · · · · · · · · · · · · · · · · · · · Makes 3 quarts

1 package Bean Soup Mix	1¼ t. salt
2 qts. water	½ t. pepper
1 Polish sausage (cut in ½" rounds)	1 large onion, chopped
1 16 oz. can chopped tomatoes	1 clove garlic, minced

♥ Rinse the beans and place in a Dutch oven. Cover with water and soak overnight. Drain water. Add 2 qts. water and remaining ingredients. Reduce heat after bringing to a boil and simmer for 2½ hours or until beans are tender. Stir occasionally. Makes 3 quarts soup. Enjoy!

THE BEST CORNBREAD

1 package cornbread mix
2 eggs
1 cup milk
½ cup butter, melted

Mix together all ingredients and pour into 8" baking pan that has been greased. Bake @ 350°F for 30 minutes

5

February

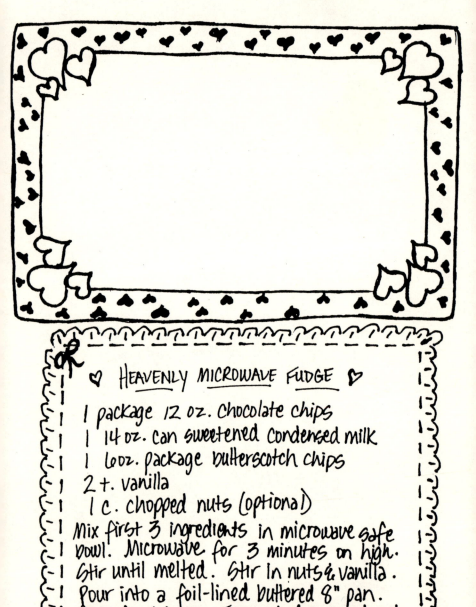

♡ HEAVENLY MICROWAVE FUDGE ♡

1 package 12 oz. chocolate chips
1 14 oz. can sweetened condensed milk
1 6 oz. package butterscotch chips
2 t. vanilla
1 c. chopped nuts (optional)

Mix first 3 ingredients in microwave safe bowl. Microwave for 3 minutes on high. Stir until melted. Stir in nuts & vanilla. Pour into a foil-lined buttered 8" pan. Chill for 1 hour. Turn out of pan and cut into squares. Makes 36 small squares.

6   MIXED WITH L♥VE!

♥ Chocolate Dipped Strawberries

Mm-mm!

1 cup chocolate chips 1 T. shortening	Melt together over low heat in double boiler stirring constantly.
1 cup white chocolate chips 1 T. shortening	Repeat above instructions.

Gently wash strawberries. Dry on paper towels or kitchen towels. Once they are dry, dip into dark chocolate. Place on a cooling rack with paper towel or waxed paper underneath to catch drips. Place melted white chocolate into a baggie. Cut off small tip of corner. Drizzle white chocolate over dipped strawberries.

Packaging IDEA!

Take a terra-cotta clay saucer and paint with white acrylic paint. Paint on tiny hearts or tiny strawberries in pinks and reds. Spray with clear acrylic spray after paint has dried. Add your fudge or chocolate dipped strawberries on a paper ♥-shaped doilie and tie up all with tulle!

MIXED WITH L♥VE! 7

Cinnamon Snack Mix

- 3 c. apple cinnamon flavored cereal
- 2 c. pecan halves
- 1 c. whole almonds
- 1 c. chow mein noodles
- 2 egg whites
- 1 c. sugar
- 2 T. cinnamon
- ½ t. salt

Preheat oven to 300°F. Mix first 4 ingredients in a large bowl. Mix next 4 ingredients and pour over nut mixture. Stir to coat well. Spread on a greased baking sheet. Bake 35-40 minutes, stirring frequently to break apart. Cool and store in air-tight container. Makes 8½ cups.

"And now these three remain: faith, hope and love. But the greatest of these is Love." 1 Corinthians 13:13

Rasberry Heart Cookies

½ c. butter, soft
1 c. sugar
1 t. baking powder
¼ t. baking soda
Dash salt
½ c. sour cream

1 egg
½ t. vanilla
½ t. almond extract
2½ c. flour
½ c. raspberry jam, seedless

Beat butter for 30 seconds with mixer. Add sugar, baking powder, baking soda and salt. Beat until combined. Stir in sour cream, egg and extracts. Mix in flour. Divide dough in half, wrap in plastic and refrigerate 2 hours. Turn out onto floured surface and roll to ⅛" thick. Using 3" ♡ cookie cutter, cut out all dough. For half of the cookies use mini ♡ cookie cutter and cut out middle. Bake @ 375°F for 7-8 minutes. Cool on wire rack. Spread jam on whole cookie shape, and top with heart shape with cut out in it. Dust with powdered sugar! Enjoy!

MIXED WITH LOVE! 9

March

Hallelujah!
He is risen;
He is risen indeed!

MIXED WITH L♥VE!

✝ HOT CROSS MUFFIN MIX ✝

1⅔ c. flour
⅔ c. sugar
2 t. baking powder
1 t. cinnamon
½ t. salt
¾ c. raisins or currants

Mix with love and place in an air-tight container. Attach label

✝ HOT CROSS MUFFINS ✝

1 package Hot Cross muffin mix
1 egg
⅓ c. oil
⅔ c. milk

TOPPING:
⅓ c. powdered sugar
2 t. milk

Mix together muffin mix, egg, oil & milk. Spoon batter into greased muffin tins filling ⅔ full. Bake @ 400°F for 20 minutes. Remove and cool on cooling rack. Mix together topping ingredients. Drizzle over muffins in shape of cross. Makes 12 muffins.

MIXED WITH LOVE! 11

March

M&M's(TM) Cookie Mix

1¼ c. flour
¼ t. salt
½ t. baking powder
⅓ c. sugar

⅓ c. brown sugar, packed
½ c. oats
½ c. crisp rice cereal
½ c. raisins
½ c. M&M's(TM) (pastel colored for Easter)

Mix all ingredients together or layer in a quart canning jar.

M&M's(TM) COOKIES

Add: 1 egg
1 t. vanilla
½ c. butter, softened

Cream together egg, vanilla & butter. Add cookie mix and combine until well-blended. Drop by rounded spoonfuls 2" apart onto a greased cookie sheet. Bake @ 350°F for 10-12 minutes. Cool on cooling rack. Makes 2½ dozen cookies.

This mix looks darling layered in a quart-size canning jar!

12 MIXED WITH LOVE!

Carrot Cake Mix

2 c. sugar
3 c. flour
2 t. baking soda
1 T. cinnamon
½ t. nutmeg
½ c. chopped nuts

Mix with love and store in an air-tight container. Attach label ⟶

CARROT CAKE

1 package carrot cake mix
1½ c. oil
3 eggs
3 c. grated carrots
1 8oz. can crushed pineapple

Pour all ingredients in a bowl and mix well. Pour into a greased 9"x13" pan and bake @ 350°F for 45-50 min. Cool the cake and frost with cream cheese frosting. Enjoy!

MIXED WITH LOVE! 13

April

Mock Devonshire Cream

1 c. heavy cream
1 T. powdered sugar
½ c. sour cream

Whip heavy cream until soft peaks form.
Blend in powdered sugar and sour cream.
Refrigerate then serve with scones
and lemon curd. Yummy!

MIXED WITH LOVE!

Friendship Tea Mix

2 c. Tang (TM) (orange-flavored drink mix)
1 c. instant iced tea (unsweetened)
1 c. sugar
¼ c. instant dry lemonade mix
1 t. cinnamon
½ t. ground cloves (optional)
¼ c. cinnamon red hot candies (optional)

Mix together all ingredients. Store in air-tight container. Attach label—

Friendship Tea Mix

Add 1-2 T. mix to 1 cup boiling water. Stir in and enjoy!
Thanks for your friendship!

Place a sealed bag of mix in a mug. Tie on a bow, label, cinnamon stick or teaspoon.

"I thank my God every time I remember you."
Philippians 1:3

"Whether near or far away,
A special friend you'll
  always be ---
When you drink this cup
  of friendship tea,
Please remember to
  think of me." Patricia Buck

MIXED WITH LOVE! 15

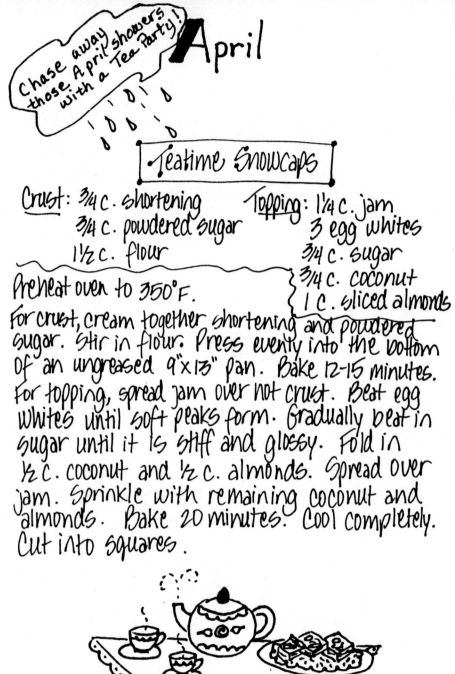

Chase away those April showers with a Tea Party!

April

Teatime Snowcaps

Crust: 3/4 c. shortening
3/4 c. powdered sugar
1 1/2 c. flour

Topping: 1 1/4 c. jam
3 egg whites
3/4 c. sugar
3/4 c. coconut
1 c. sliced almonds

Preheat oven to 350°F.

For crust, cream together shortening and powdered sugar. Stir in flour. Press evenly into the bottom of an ungreased 9"x13" pan. Bake 12-15 minutes. For topping, spread jam over hot crust. Beat egg whites until soft peaks form. Gradually beat in sugar until it is stiff and glossy. Fold in 1/2 c. coconut and 1/2 c. almonds. Spread over jam. Sprinkle with remaining coconut and almonds. Bake 20 minutes. Cool completely. Cut into squares.

MIXED WITH LOVE!

How to Brew the Perfect Pot of Tea

- ♥ Preheat the teapot by filling it with hot water and letting it stand for a few minutes.
- ♥ Fill the teakettle with cold water and bring to a boil. Cold water has more oxygen and makes a better brew.
- ♥ Place either 1 teabag or 1 teaspoon of loose tea per cup of tea.
- ♥ Pour boiling water over tea and steep 3-5 minutes. Remove teabags from tea or strain tea through a tea strainer.
- ♥ If you are serving cream and sugar, place the lumps of sugar in the teacup first, then cream, and then pour the tea over all. One calls it cream, but it really should be milk since the tannin in the tea can make the cream curdle.

"If you are cold, tea will warm you;
if you are too heated, it will cool you;
if you are depressed, it will cheer you;
if you are exhausted, it will calm you."
William Gladstone

MIXED WITH L♥VE! 17

April

♡ ♡ ♡ ♡

Teddy Bear Tea Party

- Be sure to invite your favorite teddy bears to the tea party.
- Dress up in mommy's hat, shoes, pearls and lipstick. Dress your bears up too!
- Make some bear "teawiches" with peanut butter, honey and raisins. Cut bread out with bear-shaped cutter.
- Serve with apple tea and apple cinnamon teddy bear scones. Enjoy!

"Sometimes the nicest thing about getting up is sitting down with a friend for a cup of tea."

Patricia Buck

Apricot, White Chocolate, Pecan Scones

2 c. flour
3 T. sugar
1 T. baking powder
1/4 t. salt
6 T. butter, chilled

1 egg
1/3 c. half & half
1/2 c. dried apricots
1/2 c. white chocolate chips
1/2 c. pecans, chopped

Mix together flour, sugar, baking powder and salt. Cut in butter until crumbly. Pour egg and half & half in center of dry ingredients and stir until moistened. Mix in apricots, white chocolate chips and pecans. Turn out onto a floured surface and pat down to 1/2" thickness. Cut into shapes with cookie cutter, place on baking sheet, brush with milk and sprinkle with sugar. Bake @ 400°F for 12-14 minutes. Cool on wire rack. Makes 15-18 scones. Enjoy!

May

Happy

Mother's Day

A woman's work is never done; and just about the time she thinks it is, she becomes a Grandma!

20 MIXED WITH L♥VE!

April showers bring May flowers! Make May Day baskets and hang on friend's and neighbor's doors. Decorate and line baskets with paper doilies and fill with "flower" cookies. Tuck in a rose or sprig of lilac—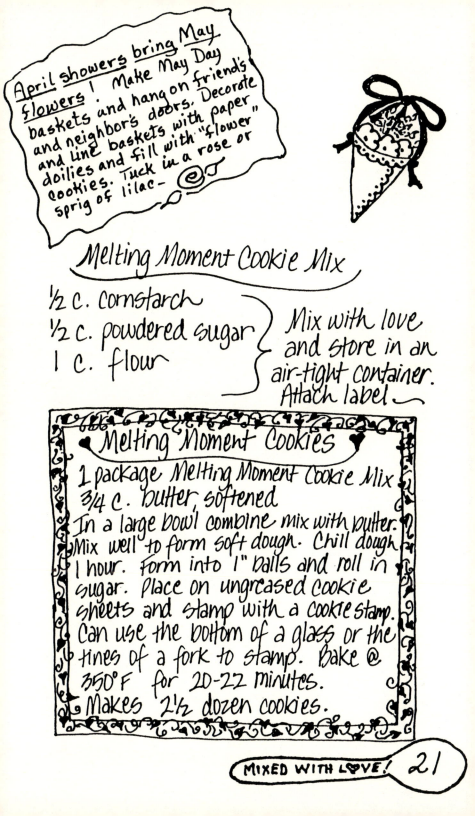

Melting Moment Cookie Mix

½ c. cornstarch
½ c. powdered sugar
1 c. flour

Mix with love and store in an air-tight container. Attach label—

Melting Moment Cookies

1 package Melting Moment Cookie Mix
¾ c. butter, softened
In a large bowl combine mix with butter. Mix well to form soft dough. Chill dough 1 hour. Form into 1" balls and roll in sugar. Place on ungreased cookie sheets and stamp with a cookie stamp. Can use the bottom of a glass or the tines of a fork to stamp. Bake @ 350°F for 20-22 minutes.
Makes 2½ dozen cookies.

IDEA

Tray for mom ~

Spray paint an old tray one of Mom's favorite colors. Kids dip hands in contrasting paint color and press on tray. Write name and date under handprints. Spray with 2-3 coats of clear acrylic spray.

Breakfast in Bed

Fresh Fruit cup
Fresh muffins
Coffee or tea
Bud vase with flower
Note to the "Best Mom in the World"

Adam
8

Amanda
6

We love you Mom!

"Her children arise and call her blessed."

Proverbs 31:28

22   MIXED WITH LOVE!

Fizzing Bath Salts

- ½ c. baking soda
- ¼ c. citric acid
- ¼ c. cornstarch
- ¾ t. fragranced oil
- 3 drops food coloring (optional)

Combine all ingredients. Place in a decorative jar and tie on label. Combine with TUB TEABAGS and a candle. Also a bath brush, loofah and washcloth is a nice addition.

Fizzing Bath Salts

Add 3 T. bath salts to bath water for a wonderful bath. Enjoy!

TUB TEABAGS

Cut a 10" square of muslin fabric and add 3 T. tea mixture to center. Tie tightly with a ribbon and make a loop. Hang under running hot bath water & enjoy!

TEA MIXTURE: Combine 1 cup each chamomile, lavendar & peppermint.

MIXED WITH LOVE! 23

May

Surprise Muffin Mix

2 c. self-rising flour
½ c. sugar
¼ c. brown sugar
1 t. cinnamon
¼ t. nutmeg

Mix with love and store in an air-tight container. Attach label

Surprise Muffins

1 package muffin mix   ¾ c. milk
1 egg   ¼ c. oil
Favorite jam

In a large bowl combine mix, egg, milk & oil. Stir until just blended. Don't overmix. Spoon batter into greased muffin tins, filling ½ full. Spoon 1 teaspoon jam onto the batter and top with more batter, filling to ¾ full. Bake @ 400°F for 15-18 minutes. Makes 12 muffins.

Idea! Treat mom to these muffins as part of a "Breakfast in Bed" tray

Lemon Curd

2/3 c. sugar
1 T. cornstarch
2 t. zest from lemon
½ c. lemon juice
¼ c. water
2 T. butter
3 beaten egg yolks

Stir together sugar and cornstarch in a medium saucepan. Add lemon zest, lemon juice, water and butter. Cook and stir over medium heat until thick. Add slowly about half of the hot lemon mixture into the beaten egg yolks. Whisk together, then pour all of the egg mixture back into the saucepan. Bring to a boil, reduce heat and cook while stirring 2 more minutes. Cover with plastic wrap and chill in refrigerator! Serve with scones and mock Devonshire cream! Enjoy!

June

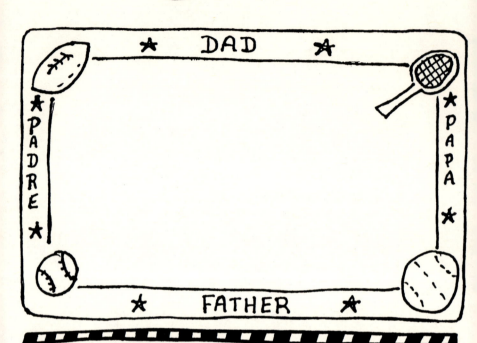

DAD · PADRE · PAPA · FATHER

BBQ Peanuts

3 c. unsalted dry roasted peanuts
⅓ c. smoke-flavored BBQ sauce
½ t. onion salt
½ t. garlic salt

In a large bowl combine all ingredients.
Mix with love! Spread on a lightly greased
baking sheet and bake @ 300°F for
20 minutes, stirring after 10 minutes.
Cool and then store in air-tight container.

26

Fiesta Spicy Snack Mix

¼ c. butter
1 pkg. Taco seasoning mix
4 c. Corn Chex℠
4 c. cheese snack crackers
2½ c. peanuts
2 c. small pretzels
2 cans French fried onions

Melt butter and mix in Taco seasoning. In a large roasting pan mix the remaining ingredients. Pour butter mixture over and mix well. Bake @ 250°F for 1 hour, stirring every 15 minutes. Cool and store in air-tight container.

CONTAINER IDEAS

- Bucket with team logo decoupaged on it.
- Plastic football helmet.
- Baseball cap.
- Favorite team shirt — stitch bottom closed and fill with bags of snack mixes.

"A good man obtains favor from the LORD." Proverbs 12:2

MIXED WITH LOVE! 27

June

Couch Potato Seasoning Mix

3 T. parsley flakes
2 T. garlic salt
2 T. seasoning salt
1 T. dried chives
1 t. black pepper

Mix together with love and store in an air-tight container.

COUCH POTATOES

Layer sliced potatoes with or without peel in greased baking dish. Dot each layer with butter and sprinkle with seasoning mix. Bake @ 350°F for 35-45 minutes. Cover with shredded cheddar cheese. Return to oven until melted. Top with sliced green onions, bacon bits & sour cream.

Gift IDEA!

- Lap top TV tray
- TV Guide
- Bag of potatoes
- Jar of Couch Potato Mix
- Big insulated mug

MIXED WITH LOVE!

BBQ Spice Mix

2 T. chili powder
2 T. cumin
½ t. oregano
1 t. garlic powder
1 t. salt
½ t. pepper
1 t. onion salt
½ t. red pepper flakes
1 t. cinnamon
½ C. brown sugar

BBQ Spices

Generously sprinkle on raw meat about 2 hours before grilling. Refrigerate and allow flavors to be absorbed. Grill or broil as desired. Especially good on pork or chicken! Enjoy!

Give mix with BBQ tongs and oven mitt!

Caramel Coconut Corn

12 C. popped popcorn
3 C. peanuts
1 C. shredded coconut
1 C. brown sugar, packed
½ C. butter
¼ C. corn syrup
½ t. salt
½ t. baking soda
1 t. vanilla

In a large bowl combine popcorn, peanuts & coconut. Combine sugar, butter, corn syrup and salt in pan. Cook over medium heat, stirring constantly. Bring to a boil and cook without stirring 5 minutes. Remove from heat and stir in baking soda and vanilla. Pour over popcorn mix stirring until coated. Divide into 2 greased 9x13 pans. Bake @ 200°F for 1 hour, stirring every 15 minutes. Cool completely and store in air-tight container. ENJOY!

MIXED WITH LOVE! 29

JULY

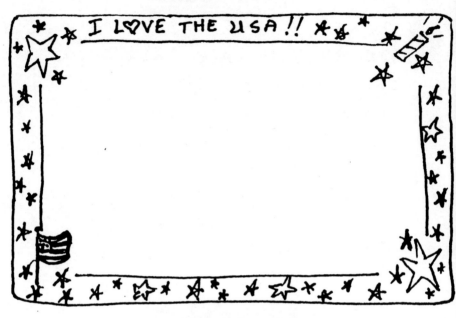

I LOVE THE USA !!

Red, White & Blue Muffins

Prepare your favorite blueberry muffin mix.
Fill muffin tins ⅓ full and then put a
spoonful of cherry, strawberry or raspberry
preserves on top of batter. Cover with
more batter to ¾ full. Bake as usual.
✮ Quick, delicious 4th of July breakfast treat!

Stardust Cookie Mix
Makes 4 mixes

5 c. flour
2 c. sugar
1 t. baking powder
½ t. salt
Red, White & Blue sugar sprinkles
4 star cookie cutters — 12 straws

* Mix first 4 ingredients together with love.
Divide evenly into 4 packages (approx. 1⅜ c.)

* Tape one end of straw and funnel colors
of sugar into each — 4 red's — 4 blue's - 4 whites.
After filling, tape the remaining end closed.

* Tie a red, white and blue ribbon around
the top, tie on the straws and star cookie
cutter. Attach the following label.

STARDUST COOKIES

1 package cookie mix   1 egg
½ c. butter, softened   1 t. vanilla
Place mix in bowl and add all ingredients. Mix well.
Chill dough for 1 hour. Roll dough out on a floured
surface to ¼" thick. Cut with ✶ cookie cutter.
Sprinkle with colored sugar and press lightly on.
Bake @ 350°F for 11-13 minutes on ungreased
cookie sheet. Remove to wire rack to cool.
Enjoy!

MIXED WITH LOVE!   31

July

★ ★ ★ ★ ★ ★ ★ ★ ★ ★ ★

Coffee Can Ice Cream

1 c. milk
1 c. whipping cream
½ c. sugar
1 t. vanilla

Crushed ice
Rock salt
1 1# coffee can
1 3# coffee can

Mix milk, cream, sugar & vanilla. Pour into clean 1# coffee can. Put lid on and tape very securely. Place 1# can into 3# can. Layer crushed ice and rock salt in 3# can around 1# can. Put lid on 3# can and seal shut with tape. Roll back and forth between 2 or more kids for 15 minutes. (Makes 4 ½ cup servings)

★ Keep a couple of sets of cans with your camping supplies. Kids of all ages love it!

Stars & Stripes Votives

Save baby food jars. Paint on stars and stripes with clear nail polish and sprinkle with colored glitter. Add a tea light or votive and set on your patio, porch, etc.

MIXED WITH LOVE!

Nutty Ice Cream Crumble

2 c. flour
1 c. butter, melted
1 c. chopped pecans
½ c. brown sugar
½ c. quick oats

> **Nutty Ice Cream Crumble**
> Sprinkle over ice cream, topped with your favorite sauce! Also good in layered parfaits.

Combine all ingredients and mix with love! Spread crumbles in an ungreased jelly roll pan. Bake @ 400°F for 15 minutes. Stir once halfway through baking. Cool and store in an air-tight container.

Quick Caramel Sauce

½ c. butter
1 14 oz. can sweetened condensed milk
1 14 oz. bag caramels

Combine ingredients in pan and cook over low heat stirring constantly until melted.
* This is good to dip sliced apples in too!

IDEA!
Give a package of Nutty ice cream crumble, a jar of Quick Caramel Sauce, ice cream dishes and of course an ice cream scoop!

August

Ice Cream Cone Cupcakes

Make 1 box of cake mix according to directions. Place cake ice cream cones into mini muffin tins. Spoon cake batter into ice cream cones and fill 2/3 full. Bake @ 375°F for 20 minutes. Frost tops of "ice cream" when cooled.

MUD PIE MIX

1 Chocolate instant pudding mix "MUD" → (4 serving size)

24 chocolate sandwich cookies finely crushed "DIRT" →

1½ C. assorted chocolate chips, peanuts, raisins, granola, etc. "ROCKS" →

"CREATURES" - assorted gummy worms, frogs, etc.

Open pudding mix and pour into package. Label "MUD". Pour cookie crumbs into package and label "DIRT". Pour assorted chocolate chips, etc. into package and label "ROCKS". Do the same for the assorted "CREATURES."
Place all of the labeled bags into the center of a purchased chocolate pie crust. Tie up with cellophane, ribbon and label.

MUD PIE

1 Mud Pie Mix	1 8oz. carton whipped
1 cup milk	topping, thawed

Pour "MUD" in bowl with 1 cup milk. Whisk until well-blended. Let stand 5 minutes. Fold in the whipped topping. Stir in 3/4 cup "DIRT" and the bag of "ROCKS." Pour into pie crust and sprinkle with remaining "DIRT." Freeze for 4 hours or until firm. Decorate with "CREATURES."   Enjoy!

August

Yo-Yo Cookies

Buy or make a batch of round sugar cookies.

Filling: Beat together 3 cups powdered sugar, 1 cup butter, 1 t. dried grated orange peel & 1 t. orange extract.

Spread filling generously on half of cookies. Top with remaining cookies. For each yo-yo string, cut a 20" length of string. Tie one end into a small loop for your finger. Wrap remaining end around cookie. Store in an air-tight container. Remove string before eating cookie.

Better to try something and fail, than to try nothing and succeed!

Hanging Lanterns

Make hanging lanterns out of ordinary canning jars. Paint on flowers, bees, butterflies, stripes or whatever on outside of jars. Wrap wire around the neck of the jar and add a wire handle. Add a votive candle or a tea light. Hang in your patio or garden. Instant party lights!

Treat your family like friends, and your friends like family.

September

TEACHER

A
B
C

A
B

C
A
T

1 2 3 4 5 6 7 8 9

Make enlarged copies of these monthly labels, color, cut out inside section and place in a plexiglass frame for a seasonal border picture mat.

Dip Me

Taffy Apple Dip

1 8oz. package cream cheese
3/4 c. brown sugar
1/4 c. powdered sugar
1 T. vanilla
1 c. chopped peanuts

Mix all ingredients with love! Serve with sliced apples.

Caramel Apple Cookie Pizza

4 large apples, sliced & dipped in lemon juice
1 tube refrigerator sugar cookie dough
8 oz. cream cheese
½ c. creamy peanut butter
6 oz. jar caramel ice cream topping
¼ c. chopped nuts

Roll out sugar cookie dough onto round pizza stone. Bake @ 350°F for 20 minutes. Let cool. Blend together cream cheese and peanut butter. Spread onto cookie. Arrange apple slices on top, drizzle with caramel sauce, and sprinkle with nuts.

Strawberry Kiwi Tea Mix

2 c. instant iced tea mix
1 pkg. strawberry kiwi drink mix (2 qt. size)
Combine and store in air-tight container.

Strawberry Kiwi Tea
Stir 1 T. mix into
8 oz. hot or cold water.
Mix and enjoy!

MIXED WITH LOVE! 39

September

Magic Growing Pancake Mix

1 cup flour
1/4 cup sugar
1 t. cinnamon

Mix with love and place in air-tight container— Attach label and add a bottle of wonderful maple syrup!

Magic Growing Pancakes

1 package Magic Growing Pancake Mix
1/3 C. butter
4 eggs
1 c. milk

"It's Magic"

Preheat oven to 425°F. Place butter in a 9" oven proof pie plate. Set pie plate in oven to melt butter. Pour pancake mix, milk and eggs in bowl and whisk together. Pour batter onto the butter and bake 20-25 minutes. Serve immediately with powdered sugar, syrup and/or sliced berries. Wow! It grew!

40   MIXED WITH LOVE!

Peanut Butter Brownie Mix

½ C. sugar
½ C. brown sugar
½ C. flour
½ t. baking powder
½ t. salt

Mix all ingredients
with love!
Pour into an
air-tight package!
Attach label—

Peanut Butter Brownies

1 package Peanut Butter Brownie Mix
2 eggs
¼ C. butter, softened
½ C. peanut butter
Place brownie mix into bowl and mix
with eggs and butter. Blend in
peanut butter. Pour into 9"x9" baking
pan. Bake @ 350°F for 20-25 minutes.
Cool and cut into squares. Enjoy!

TEACHER GIFT!

Idea

Paint a large can with
chalkboard flat black paint.
Paint on "chalk" with white
paint. Fill with a mix, tea
and a cute mug. Tie on a
label.

41

October

Chocolate Spider Web Pizza

1 12oz. package chocolate chips
1 cup peanuts
1 cup candy corn

Line a 9" cake pan with plastic wrap. Melt chocolate chips in a sauce pan over low heat stirring constantly. Remove from heat and stir in peanuts. Pour into pan. Press candy corn into chocolate. Cool to room temperature. Remove from pan and peel away plastic wrap. Cut into wedges to serve.

42

Pumpkin Pie Spice Mix

¼ c. cinnamon
2 T. ground ginger
1 T. nutmeg
1 T. cloves
1 T. allspice

Mix with love and store in an air-tight container. Makes ½ cup mix.

Pumpkin Pie

2 c. canned pumpkin
2 eggs
¾ c. sugar
1½ t. pumpkin pie spice mix
1⅔ c. light cream
1 9" piecrust, unbaked

Mix first 5 ingredients together until smooth. Pour into unbaked piecrust and bake @ 425°F for 15 minutes. Reduce heat to 350°F and continue baking 45 minutes. Serve with whipped cream! Yummy!

October

Chocolate Spiders

8 oz. semi-sweet chocolate chips
2 c. mini marshmallows
Black shoestring licorice
48 M&M's™

In a microwave bowl, heat chocolate for 2 minutes @ 50% power, stirring after 1 minute. Stir until melted. Let stand 5 minutes. Stir in marshmallows. Drop by tablespoonfuls onto waxed paper lined baking sheets. Cut licorice into 2" pieces. Press 4 pieces into 2 sides of mounds for spider legs. Press 2 M&M's™ into each for eyes. Refrigerate until firm. Makes 24 spiders.

you can't scare me...
I have kids!

MIXED WITH LOVE!

Pumpkin Cheese Ball

1 8oz. package cream cheese
½ C. canned pumpkin
1 8oz. can crushed pineapple, drained
2 C. shredded cheddar cheese
1 T. chopped onion
½ t. seasoning salt
½ C. chopped pecans

Beat cream cheese, pumpkin and pineapple together. Stir in cheese, onion, salt and pecans. Shape into a ball and place on serving plate. Score sides with a knife to look like ribs on pumpkin. Add celery leaves for stem. Serve with veggies and crackers.

October

Chocolate Potion

1 15 oz. can sweetened condensed milk
1 4 oz. German sweet chocolate bar
1 cup whipping cream, whipped
1 t. vanilla

Mix milk and chocolate in small sauce pan over low heat, stirring constantly until chocolate melts. Cool to room temperature. Fold in whipped cream and vanilla. Use immediately or store in refrigerator.

Add ¼ c. chocolate potion to mug. Add ½ c. hot milk and stir to blend. Try it in coffee too!

Mmm-Mmm Chocolate!

A "hug" delights and warms and charms -- it must be why God gave us arms.

Mulling Spice Mix

2 cinnamon sticks, broken
6 whole cloves
6 whole allspice
1 T. orange peel, dried
2   4"x6" pieces of cheesecloth

Combine spices and tie up inside 2 layers of cheesecloth.

MULLING SPICES

1 gallon apple cider
4 T. brown sugar
1 bundle mulling spices

Pour apple cider into a large sauce pan. Add brown sugar & bundle. Simmer until flavors are well-blended. Remove spice bundle & serve!

Invisible Ink Trick

Write messages with invisible ink. Let your family and friends decode your secret messages.

You need: Lemon juice, Toothpick, White typing paper
Lamp with 75 watt bulb

Dip toothpick in lemon juice and write out the message on paper. Dip in lemon juice often. Let dry. Hold paper up to a hot light bulb being very careful not to touch it. The lemon juice will turn brown and the secret message will appear!

November

Count your Blessings

Microwave Rocky Road

2 8 oz. bars milk chocolate, cut up
3 c. mini marshmallows
¾ c. chopped nuts

Place chocolate in bowl and microwave on 50% power for 2 minutes or until chocolate is melted. Stir as needed. Add nuts and marshmallows and stir. Spread in a buttered 8" square pan. Chill. Cut in squares. Enjoy!

Thanksgiving Cranberry Jell-O Salad

1 large Jell-O (cherry, strawberry or raspberry)
2 c. boiling water
1 can jellied cranberry sauce
1 16oz. tub sour cream

Dissolve Jell-O in boiling water. Pour into blender and add cranberry sauce and sour cream. Blend until smooth. Pour into Jell-O mold and chill until firm. (4 Generation Family Favorite)

This isn't just a turkey,
  As anyone can see -
I made it with my hand,
  Which is a part of me.
It comes with lots of Love
  Especially to say,
I hope you have
  a very happy
Thanksgiving day!

MIXED WITH LOVE! 49

November

Pumpkin Cranberry Bread Mix

1⅛ c. flour
1 c. sugar
1 t. baking powder
¼ t. salt
½ t. cinnamon
¼ t. nutmeg
¼ t. allspice

Add ½ c. dried cranberries on top of flour mixture.

Mix with love and place in an air-tight container. Attach label ~

Pumpkin Cranberry Bread

1 package Pumpkin Cranberry Bread mix
1 c. canned pumpkin
1 egg
¼ c. oil

Place mix in bowl and add pumpkin, egg and oil. Mix well. Pour batter into a greased 9"x5" loaf pan. Bake @ 350°F for 55-60 minutes. Cool in pan for 5-10 minutes then remove to cooling rack to finish cooling. Enjoy!

MIXED WITH LOVE!

Poultry Seasoning Mix

3 T. dried parsley
1 T. rosemary
1 T. onion powder
2 T. sage
1 T. marjoram
1 t. black pepper
1 T. seasoning salt

Mix with love and place in an air-tight container. Attach label

Poultry Seasoning

Mix 2 tablespoons of poultry seasoning mix with ½ c. butter. Rub on the outside of poultry before roasting. Mm-good!

"Give thanks to the LORD, for He is good."

Psalm 107:1

MIXED WITH LOVE! 51

December

Joy to the World!

Applesauce Cinnamon Ornaments

1½ c. cinnamon
1 c. applesauce, smooth

Mix ingredients together and roll out to ⅛"–¼" thickness. Cut out with cookie cutters. Make a hole in the top with a straw. Let dry overnight. String with ribbon and hang on tree, garlands or use as a fragrant package tie-on.

❧ Gingerbread Cookie Mix ❧

¾ c. brown sugar
2⅔ c. flour
1 t. baking soda
¼ t. salt
2 t. ginger
¾ t. cinnamon
¼ t. nutmeg
¼ t. allspice

Mix with love and place in an air-tight container. Attach label and gingerbread man cookie cutter!

Gingerbread Man Cookies

1 package gingerbread cookie mix
½ c. butter, softened
1 egg
¼ c. molasses

Cream the butter, egg & molasses. Add the cookie mix to creamed mixture and mix by hand. Roll dough out on a floured surface to ¼" thick. Cut out with cookie cutter. Bake @ 350°F for 10-14 minutes on greased cookie sheet. Decorate as desired! Enjoy!

53

December

In the Kitchen with Grandma Party

♥ Plan a day during the holidays to spend with your grandchildren. Even better, have them overnight too! (This is the mommy's idea ☺!) Rent a favorite holiday movie and order out pizza! Maybe even go to pick out your Christmas tree together and decorate it. The next morning it's to the kitchen we go! Make gingerbread men cookies, chocolate dipped pretzels (and fingers ☺), and ice cream cone angels. Make mixes for them to take home to give to their friends and neighbors. Have fun making warm fuzzy memories!

P.S. Take lots of pictures!

54   MIXED WITH L♥VE!

Ice Cream Cone Angels

Cookie head
Lifesaver halo
Coconut hair (tint yellow)
Pretzel wings
Frost sugar cone
Sprinkle w/ colored
Sugar

Use frosting to "glue"
it all together —

"Angels we have heard
  on high,
Sweetly singing..."

The Christmas Angel

"For behold, I bring you good news of a
great joy which shall be for all the people;
for today in the city of David there has
been born for you a Savior, who is
Christ the Lord."

Luke 2:10-11

Chocolate-Dipped Anything

1 12 oz. package chocolate chips
1 T. shortening

Melt chocolate and shortening in a double boiler over <u>very low</u> heat stirring constantly.

<u>Dipping</u> ideas: Cinnamon sticks, peppermint sticks, pretzels, pretzel rods, raisins, dried fruits, Oreos™ graham crackers, etc.

Sprinkle with colored sugar or other cake decorating goodies. Place on a wire cooling rack with paper underneath to catch drippings! Easy clean-up ☺. Chill and pack in air-tight containers.

Everything tastes better with chocolate! Yum!

No-Bake Brownies

1 14 oz. can sweetened condensed milk
1 box (12oz.) vanilla wafer cookies, crushed
½ C. chopped nuts
1 oz. unsweetened baking chocolate, melted
½ C. chocolate chips, melted

In a large bowl mix first 4 ingredients. Spread into a greased 9" round cake pan. Spread melted chocolate chips over top, cover and refrigerate 1 hour or until firm. Cut into wedges and serve.

Baby Food Jar Snowglobes

Clean jars and lids of baby food jars. Glue on inside of lid little plastic Christmas trees, snowmen or angels. Fill jar with water and a couple of drops of glycerin. Add some glitter. Attach lid on and secure or glue tightly. Let your children shake them up. They can also put stickers on the outside too!

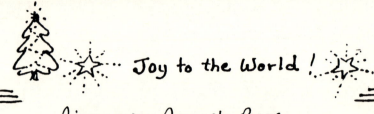

Cinnamon Crunch Bars

12 cinnamon graham crackers
2 c. chopped nuts
1 c. butter
1 c. brown sugar, packed
½ t. cinnamon

Preheat oven to 400°F. Place graham crackers in a single layer with sides touching in bottom of a foil-lined 10"x15" jelly roll pan. Sprinkle nuts evenly over crackers. Combine butter, brown sugar & cinnamon in a sauce pan. Stir constantly over medium heat until it comes to a boil. Boil 3 minutes w/o stirring. Pour over crackers and bake 8-10 minutes until bubbly and dark around edges. Cool in pan then break into pieces. Store in air-tight container.

Snowman Cookie Mix

2 c. flour
¾ c. sugar
¼ t. baking powder

} Mix with love and place in an air-tight package. Attach label.

Optional small package:
  Include small package of red hots, chocolate chips and candy corn.

Snowman Cookies

1 package Snowman Cookie mix
¾ c. butter, softened
1 egg
1 t. vanilla

Mix all ingredients together. Wrap dough in plastic and chill for 30 minutes. Roll about 1½ T. of dough into a 10" rope. On an ungreased cookie sheet coil rope up into an S. Repeat with remaining dough. Place 3 red hots for buttons, 2 mini chocolate chips for eyes and 3 more for mouth. A small candy corn can be used for nose. Bake @ 375°F for 12-15 minutes.

Clay Pot Baking

♥Creatively welcome family and friends to the scent of homemade bread baking in these garden containers.

Terra-Cotta 3-Tier Rolls

2   4-inch new clay pots
1   8-inch new clay saucer
1   10-inch new clay saucer
1   6-inch new clay saucer
2 packages frozen bread dough rolls, thawed
Parchment paper
Cooking spray
1 egg
1 T. water
Toppings: Oats, poppy seeds, sesame seeds, fennel seeds.

God gives us the ingredients for our daily bread, but He expects us to do the baking!

- Spray all pots and saucers with cooking spray. Line all saucers with parchment and spray parchment. Invert 4" pot into middle of 10" saucer. Arrange 20 rolls around pot. Invert 4" pot into middle of 8" saucer. Arrange 12 rolls around pot. Arrange 8 rolls on 6" saucer. Cover and let rise until doubled.
- Whisk together egg and water. Brush on top of each roll and sprinkle with desired toppings.
- Bake @ 375°F for 20 minutes. You may need foil to shield rolls from browning too much. Cool on wire racks. Run a sharp knife to loosen rolls from edge of saucer. Stack 6" and 8" saucers on top of pots to achieve 3-tier centerpiece.

♥ BAKING IN CLAY POTS ♥

Line terra-cotta pots with parchment paper and spray with vegetable cooking spray. Fill ½ full with bread dough, let rise and then bake.

1 6" pot — 1 loaf — 20 min. rise — 25 min. bake
1 9"x5" planter — 2 loaves — 1 hour 15 min. rise — 40 min. bake
375°F Baking temperature

MIXED WITH LOVE! 61

৬~ Very V-licious Vanilla ~৩

Vanilla Bean Extract

To make your own homemade vanilla, simply take 3 vanilla beans, cut down middle, spread bean open and scrape out seeds. Place seeds and whole vanilla beans into a glass jar or bottle. Pour vodka over beans and fill to top. Place in a dark cool place for 3-4 weeks. Use your homemade vanilla as you would in your normal cooking and baking.

Vanilla Bean Oil

Take a vanilla bean, split and scrape out seeds. Place into vegetable oil and shake it up. This is great for baking that calls for oil.

Vanilla Sugar

Pour 2 cups sugar and one whole vanilla bean into food processor. Process until it is ground up with sugar. Pour into sugar shakers and tie a ribbon around it. This is wonderful in coffee, tea or sprinkled on French toast.

Colored Sugar

Shake 1/4 c. sugar in a jar with 2-3 drops of food coloring. Make several colors and put into recycled spice jars. Paint lids color of sugar.

gift Idea!

Put several jars of colored sugar and vanilla sugar in a basket with a few cookie cutters. Include a sugar cookie mix. Great for the holidays!

MIXED WITH LOVE! 63

Kibbles Kid Chow

1 c. chocolate chips
½ c. butter
½ c. creamy peanut butter
½ t. cinnamon
8 c. round toasted oat cereal
2-3 c. powdered sugar

Melt chocolate chips and butter over low heat, stirring constantly. Remove from heat and add peanut butter and cinnamon. Stir until smooth. Place cereal in large bowl and pour chocolate mixture over it. Stir until evenly coated. Put powdered sugar into large paper bag. Pour cereal in and SHAKE! Shake until coated with sugar. Spread on waxed paper and allow to dry completely. Store in air-tight container.

IDEA: SERVE in a new clean doggie dish—or give a bag with a big bow tied around it in a new doggie dish and attach bone label above — Kibbles Kid Chow

Party Mix for Kids

2 T. butter, melted
¼ t. cinnamon
4 c. popped corn
1 c. bite-sized grahams or animal crackers
½ c. candy-coated peanut butter candy pieces

Stir together butter & cinnamon. Pour over popcorn in large bowl. Mix with love! Add the rest of the ingredients and stir!

Kids Trail Mix

2 c. graham cereal
1 c. tiny marshmallows
1 c. peanuts
½ c. M&M's™
½ c. candy-coated peanut butter pieces
½ c. raisins

Mix all with love and store in an air-tight container!

Clay For Kids

1 c. flour
2 c. salt
Enough water to make it workable.
Mix with love! Find a kid & have fun!

Dough to Play With

2½ c. flour
½ c. salt
1 T. powder alum
2 packages unsweetened fruit
   drink mix
2 T. oil
2 c. boiling water

Mmm! Smells good!

Mix together first four ingredients.
Add oil. Pour boiling water over all
and mix well. Knead until it's
the right consistency. Keep in
a plastic zipper bag.

Containers — Containers — Containers

Almost anything that can hold something can be painted, decoupaged, sponged and decorated into a one-of-a-kind container for your gift giving — RECYCLE!

Cans — They look great painted, sponged, crackle-finished, or a nail-punched design. Punch holes in can and thread a wire through for a handle, or tie-on a twine or ribbon handle.

Paper Handle Bags — Cut out shapes in fabric and iron-on with fusible webbing. Trim with ribbon, raffia, stickers, labels, buttons, etc. Stencil, stamp or handpaint designs on the bag. Punch two holes in top of bag and tie with ribbon or raffia. Cut out windows and back with cello so your contents peek through.

Jars — Favorite containers for food! Great for mixes, candy, potpourri, candles, etc. Canning jars look good with a piece of fabric tied onto lid with ribbon. Spray paint lids of old jars to cover up writing. Decorate with buttons, old wooden spools, charms, small-toys, flowers. Spice jars and baby food jars make great containers for seasoning mixes.

- Half-pint jars — 1 cup of mix
- Pint jars — 2 cups of mix
- Quart jars — 4 cups of mix

MIXED WITH LOVE! 67

More container ideas:

- galvinized tin buckets
- potato chip cans
- paint buckets
- baskets
- old TV trays
- plates
- cups and saucers
- mugs
- plastic tubs
- laundry baskets
- aprons with pockets
- hats of all kinds
- garden gloves
- mittens
- fish bowls
- wooden boxes & crates
- metal wastebaskets
- old single saltshakers
- old pie tins
- maple sap buckets
- empty 6-pack containers

⌒ More Containers ⌒

Photocopies - Make copies of old seed packets, photos of the family, postcards, sheet music, child's artwork, etc. Make sure copyrights are no longer applicable. These copies can be cut-out and decoupaged onto containers.

Paper Shredders - Shred the Sunday funnies or the stock market pages. Use as filler in your gift containers. Brown grocery sacks or colored magazine pages work too!

Fabric Bags - Cut a 20"x12" piece of fabric. Fold in half and stitch up side and bottom with right sides facing together. Sew on grosgrain ribbon on back middle. Perfect re-usable gift bag!

Clay pots - Love these all painted up. Paint on stripes, plaids, flowers, bees, lady bugs and roses.

Peppermint Candy - Take two cake rounds, (the cardboard rounds found in cake decorating stores), draw peppermint stripes on with red marker. Place cookies, biscotti, shortbread or your favorite in-between the cake rounds, tie up with cellophane and tie on big red ribbons. So cute!

MIXED WITH LOVE! 69

Theme Gifts

♥ When thinking of gift giving, try to think of the one receiving the gift. Use a theme centered around their hobbies or likes. They will feel loved because of your thoughtfulness!

Tea Party Theme- Use a large wire cup & saucer or a basket, filling it with a scone mix, flavored tea, decorated sugar cubes, teaspoon, a pretty hankie or lacey napkins, and a pair of teapot earrings.

Family Gifts- Fill a large popcorn tub, bowl or basket with snack mix, cookie mix, hot chocolate mix, favorite video, puzzle or game.

Welcome Neighbor- A basket with freshly baked cookies with Friendship Tea Mix, list of neighbors, and a list of some of your favorite local merchants.

Sports Fan- Sew up bottom of a favorite team T-shirt closed. Fill up the shirt with snack mix, popcorn, candy, softballs and sports trading cards.

Index

Index

Index

Notes

Notes

Sheryl Lynn's
4349 Clearwood Road
Moorpark, CA 93021
805/523-0900

HOW
TO
ORDER

I would like to order:

HOW
MANY?

_____ Mommy & Me in the Kitchen @ $9.95 $ _____ .

CA residents add 7.25% — $ _____
Sales tax

Shipping/Handling $2.00 EA — $ _____

Prices subject to change.   TOTAL — $ _____
Checks, money orders, VISA, Mastercard accepted.

Charge # _____
Expiration _____

Ship to: _____
Address: _____
City: _____   State: ___   Zip: _____
Phone #: _____